Writing a Letter

Kathleen Wood and Ian Forsyth

Designed by Richard Hollis and illustrated by Posy Simmonds

Nelson/The Post Office

Thomas Nelson and Sons Ltd
Lincoln Way Windmill Road
Sunbury-on-Thames Middlesex TW16 7HP
PO Box 73146 Nairobi Kenya
308–312 Lockhart Road Golden
Coronation Building 2nd Floor Blk A
Hong Kong
116–D JTC Factory Building
Lorong 3 Geylang Square Singapore 14
Thomas Nelson Australia Pty Ltd
19–39 Jeffcott Street
West Melbourne Victoria 3003

Thomas Nelson and Sons (Canada) Ltd
81 Curlew Drive Don Mills Ontario

Thomas Nelson (Nigeria) Ltd
8 Ilupeju Bypass PMB 21303 Ikeja Lagos

First published 1971
in association with
The Post Office

Reprinted 1972, 1975, 1977, 1978,
1979 (twice)

ISBN 0 17 433010 3

Printed in Hong Kong

Acknowledgements   Thanks are due to
Jonathan Cape Ltd for permission to reproduce
the extract from *Roots*, by Arnold Wesker, to
Martin Secker and Warburg Ltd and
Miss Sonia Brownell for George Orwell's
letter from *Collected Essays, Journals and Letters
of George Orwell*, and to Methuen and Co. Ltd
for the extracts from *German Students'
War Letters*, edited by A. F. Wedd.

Contents

Letters of thanks, letters from banks,
Letters of joy from girl and boy,
Receipted bills and invitations
To inspect new stock and visit relations,
And applications for situations,
And timid lovers' declarations,
And gossip, gossip from all the nations,
News circumstantial, news financial,
Letters with holiday snaps to enlarge in,
Letters with faces all scrawled in the margin,
Letters from uncles, cousins and aunts,
Letters to Scotland from the South of France,
Letters of condolence from Highlands to Lowlands,
Notes from overseas to the Hebrides;
Written on paper of every hue,
The pink, the violet, the white and the blue;
The chatty, the catty, the boring, adoring,
The cold and official and the heart's outpouring.
Clever, stupid, short and long,
The typed and the printed and the spelt all wrong.

from 'Night Mail' by W. H. Auden

Introduction

Whether you send a letter or pick up the telephone is not merely a matter of convenience or personal preference. There are occasions when the letter is the most effective means of getting something done; a letter of complaint is more likely to get results than any number of irate phone calls. In some situations, a letter may be obligatory: the letter accepting a job and its conditions is confirmation of a legal contract between employer and employee.

In both examples, as indeed in all cases, the letter stands as a relatively permanent record which may be referred to as the situation demands.

Besides this, what marks out the letter most particularly from all other means of communication is that it allows us to choose between the extremes of the intimate personal style we adopt with close friends and the formal and impersonal style of business correspondence.

There are two basic questions when we write a letter: 'Who am I writing to?' and, 'Why am I writing?'

The answers to both these questions will determine <u>what</u> we write and also <u>how</u> we write it. You might, for instance, be writing to a friend telling him what a good time you're having on holiday, or you might be writing to him as Secretary of a Sports Club to give notice of your resignation from the committee. Although the same person is involved, you would no doubt write two very different letters, the second of which would be the more formal.

As we examine different types of letters, we shall note that various conventional devices are used to indicate the appropriate degree of formality.

General Instructions

Choice of paper

Purple ink on green paper may suit your own artistic tastes, but will it bring pleasure or discomfort to the eyes of your reader? Of course, certain kinds of paper may be used deliberately to achieve a particular result. A father, who received from his young soldier son a letter written on paper torn from a War Department toilet-roll, at once took the point of his son's poverty-stricken state and sent him a sum of money! But for most occasions plain white, blue, or grey, unlined paper is the most suitable.

Layout

Aim at leaving space at each edge of the page so that the actual writing appears to be in a frame. Apart from its pleasing appearance this enables letters to be filed without any of their contents being masked.

You will see from the handwritten letters in the book that they all begin with the sender's address written at the top right-hand side of the paper so that it slopes diagonally from left to right.

The date is written below the address.

Note also the positioning of the salutation (greeting) and the subscription (ending).

Handwriting

Handwriting reflects our age, sex, personality, and changing moods, and it would be misleading to think that it could, or ever should, be as uniform and impersonal as typing. Nevertheless we always have to think of the receiver of the letter and aim at total legibility so that the letter may be read smoothly and not as if it were a series of codes to be deciphered.

There is no hard and fast rule which says some letters must be typed and others not, but for general convenience, speed, and the taking of a carbon copy, business letters are usually typed, and it is a matter of good manners that thankyou letters and letters of sympathy are hand-written.

The Envelope

Care must be given to the accurate addressing of the envelope so that the letter may be safely and speedily delivered.

The envelope may be set out in two ways:

a.   with each line indented:

```
        Mr W Brown
          17 Duff Street
           MACDUFF
            Banffshire
              AB4 1TL
```

b.   with each line starting at the same point:

```
    R. H. Cavill, Esq.
    Layne's Mfg. Co. Ltd.
    200 Upper Rushton Road
    BRADFORD
    Yorkshire
    BD3 7LQ
```

The second is often used in type-written addresses, particularly where the address contains one or more very long lines.

Whichever way you choose, remember:

1   To leave enough room at the top for the stamp to be franked without the post-mark covering up part of the address.

2   Never omit
(a)   the name of the person and/or title of the business,
(b)   the number of the house or building,
(c)   the street or road name,
(d)   the district, when the town or village is not well known, e.g. Stow-Cum-Quy, Cambridge-shire,
(e)   the district, when there is more than one town of the same name, e.g. Bradford, Yorkshire, Bradford-on-Avon, Wiltshire. (These are just two of the six towns of this name in the U.K. A Postcode eases this confusing situation.)

3   Print the name of the post town in BLOCK CAPITALS.

4   If the address has a Post-code, use it. This code appears on the last line of the address and is always written without punctuation and in block capitals. Correct use of the Postcode speeds sorting as it becomes ever increasingly automatic.

5   To aid automatic sorting, the Post Office will probably, in the near future, ask that the punctuation used on the envelope should be restricted to the name, and that commas and full-stops should be omitted from the other lines of the address.

1 Between Friends Personal Letters

The first kind of letter that we look at is the wholly personal letter as between friends and relations.

When do you send this kind of letter? Probably when you are staying away from home and not seeing friends for quite a long time. And why do you write letters in these circumstances? Sometimes, certainly, it's to make a request or to pass on a special piece of news. Often, though, it's a matter of keeping in touch, of maintaining a relationship between you and the person to whom you are writing.

You are writing in an informal situation to a person you know well, so restricting influences should be very few. Yet difficulties are still experienced in writing such a letter.

✉ **Examine the following letter from a soldier in Hong Kong. It tells his mother he is well, but we learn little of what he thinks about life in another country and hardly any of Angus's personality is revealed in the letter.**

23456789 Gnr. A. McTavish, R.A.,
Q Battery,
99 Medium Regt, R.A.,
B.F.P.O. 1
23rd March 1979

Dear Mum,
   Just a few lines to let you know that everything is O.K. at this end. I hope all at home are fit and well. Things are quiet here as usual, just the odd parade and guard duty once a fortnight. The Christmas pudding you sent arrived last month, and we all enjoyed the mince pies. Some of them had a bit of mould on the edges, but most of them were O.K. Well, Mum, roll on Summer. Only three months before I'm home again.
      Keep smiling,
         Angus

▣➤ **Now put yourself in Angus's place and try to improve on his letter. Bear the following in mind when you are preparing your version:**

1 Neither Angus nor any of his family had ever been abroad before he was posted to Hong Kong.

2 There will be many contrasts between life at home and in South-east Asia; people, climate, food, and so on.

9

Look at part of a letter written on 26 December 1938 to Jack Common from the writer, George Orwell, in Marrakech, Morocco.

Unlike Angus, writing from Hong Kong, Orwell can write interestingly about even such a commonplace subject as the weather.

➡ Make a list of all the other subjects which he writes about in this passage.

You asked where Marrakech was. It's somewhere near the top left-hand corner of Africa and immediately north of the Atlas Mountains. Funnily enough we've been having the cold snap even here and on Christmas Eve there was a heavy frost – don't know whether that is usual here, but judging by the vegetation I don't think it can be. I had the queer and rather pleasant experience of seeing the oranges and lemons on the trees frosted all over, which apparently didn't damage them. The effects of the frost were very curious. Some nasturtiums I had sown earlier were withered up by it, but the cactuses and the Bougainvillea, which is a tropical plant from the South Pacific, weren't affected. The mountains have been covered with snow even on their lower slopes for some time past. As soon as I've done the rough draft of my novel we're going to take a week off and go into the mountains. The Romans thought they were the end of the world, and they certainly look as if they might be. It's generally fine and bright in the daytime, but we have fires all the time. The only fuel is olive wood, because there simply isn't a wild tree for miles and miles. This is one of those countries which are very nearly desert and which just exactly support a small population of men and beasts who eat every eatable thing and burn every burnable thing on the surface, so that if there were one more person there'd be a famine. And to think that in Roman times North Africa was full of magnificent forests full of lions and elephants. There are now practically no wild animals bigger than a hare, and I suppose even the human population is smaller.

Nothing to Say?

In the following extract from the play Roots, by Arnold Wesker, Beattie is showing her annoyance and frustration at her inability to write a letter which does more than maintain contact between her mother and herself. She says to her mother:

66 Do you know when I used to work at the holiday camp and I sat down with the other girls to write a letter we used to sit and discuss what we wrote about. An' we all agreed, all on us, that we started: 'Just a few lines to let you know', and then we got on to the weather and then we got stuck so we write about each other and after a page an' half of big scrawl end up: 'Hoping this finds you as well as it leaves me'. There! We couldn't say any more. Thousands of things happening at this holiday camp and we couldn't find words for them. All of us the same. 99

➤ Write the letter home from the holiday camp that you think Beattie would have liked to send.

Note that your letter should be set out properly, with address, date, etc. Before you write the letter decide:
1 What Beattie's particular job would be—waitress, cook, chalet-maid, children's nurse, etc.
2 What would her mother worry over and like to hear about— staff meals, sleeping quarters, laundering facilities, friends Beattie makes, etc?
3 How may Beattie's own personality be shown—is she a moaner, forgetful, talkative, accident-prone, lazy, etc?

11

Plenty to Say

✉ **The following letter appears
to give quite a lot of information,
but do you find it satisfactory?**

3 Market Avenue
Brighouse
Yorkshire
HD6 4JS

March 20th 1979

Dear Linda,

Yesterday I went with the school trip to London
to see the Ideal Home Exhibition.

Mum got me up at half past six and I managed
to bolt down a huge breakfast of cornflakes, egg, bacon,
tomatoes, toast and two cups of coffee.

At 7.30 I caught the bus to school. The coach which
was to take us to London arrived at five minutes past
eight and, when all thirty-eight of us were aboard,
it left at 8.30. I sat on the back seat with Penny
Francis, Betty Webb, Rosemary Winder and Heather Stacey. As
soon as we'd left Sheffield we started singing and
eating crisps and sweets.

We stopped at a Motorway café at 10.30 until 11.
We reached London at one o'clock when Miss Hazeldean had
arranged for us to have lunch in a restaurant.

When we got to the Exhibition we seemed to walk for
miles. I liked the stone built show house, and the stands
displaying Dairy Produce, wallpaper and carpets.

We set off back at half past five after tea and sang
all the way home. We got back to school at 10.15 and
Dad picked me up in the car. I went straight to bed and
didn't wake till 10 this morning. I must finish now
as I'm going shopping with Mum this afternoon.

Write soon and tell me your news.
                    Love,
                    Pat

Has the writer given the letter any central point? If not, what do you think should provide the main point of interest?

There are two kinds of repetition used in the letter. What are they, and what effect do they have on your appreciation of the letter?

Now write:

1 ▸ A letter on a similar theme in which you pay a visit to either a sporting event, a factory, a newspaper printing press, or the theatre. Think where the focus of your letter will lie.

2 ▸ Two letters to a pen-friend: one is the first letter you write to start the correspondence; the second is when you have been writing to each other for a year.

Why should one expect the first one to be more formal than the second?

Note. The choice of endings in these personal letters is fairly unrestricted. As a general rule, however, if you are writing to a person you don't really know intimately, 'Yours sincerely' is the most suitable choice.

What Shall I Tell Them?

✉ **These extracts are taken from letters written by four German students who served in the First World War.**

✠ Armed with the heavy hand-pump we started. It was a lovely night. The full moon shone in the sky and lit up the way, which on a dark night is hard to find owing to the many trenches and wire-entanglements. The Frenchies were keeping comparatively quiet, and only now and then was the report of a rifle and a bullet whizzed by, or a missile struck a tree, ricocheted and flew on with a melancholy note. Also as it was bright moonlight very few flares went up. Far away on the left, probably near Ypres, the thunder of guns growled. Otherwise all was still. Soundlessly we proceeded over the duck-boards along the narrow trench. When we reached the wet place the work began. My men took hold valiantly, and as there had been but little rain during the previous few days, the trench was soon pumped dry. Suddenly one of the men said: 'Hello, there's the pear-tree which the stretcher bearers said was chock full of ripe pears!' And before I could stop them, the chaps had jumped out of the trench and begun – only 120 yards from the enemy – to pelt the tree with bits of stick and lumps of clay! Imagine the scene – here in the moonlight, close to the enemy, those foolhardy devils running round with no cover, while bullets were whistling all about them, shying at pears! Certainly they were screened from observation by a fine white mist which was lying over the land. In a few minutes they had got every single pear off the tree, and, loaded with fruit, we started back.

✠ To-day I have to go in for my first exam. – that of Pilot. I have to do all sorts of things in the air – make an '8', various landings, etc. Everybody here is astonished at my being already so far advanced and flying so well alone after only four weeks. I find it tremendous sport. Since I have been able to fly alone I have the sole use of a simply perfect machine – an Albatross bi-plane, with a 100-h.p. Mercedes engine. A few days ago I was about 4,000 ft. up and about 1,000 ft. above the clouds, in the evening towards sunset. Down below, on the earth, the weather was dull and unpleasant, but it was a glorious sight when I rose out of the gloomy region below into the most gorgeous sunshine above the clouds which lay like an endless shroud over the earth. One could quite forget that somewhere down there was a world where miserable human beings were crawling about. I felt as if I could easily step out of my aeroplane and walk about on the clouds (I didn't try, however). It was quite unearthly. I pity the people who can't have such an experience. I should like to take you all up with me one day.

✠ 'What on earth are we at?' I whisper to my neighbours. 'How should I know?' one answers; the other is asleep. Well, I settle myself down as comfortably as I can. It just happens not to have rained that day, and we are lying in a fairly dry spot. 'The troops will advance, cloth-touching! Pass it along!' *'The troops will advance, cloth-touching! Pass it along!'* 'Order received! Order received!' (All in a whisper.)

(If only one knew, Neighbour, what we are to do when we get to the enemy – are we to hop into the trench and whack around, or stand on the edge and bang at him, or what?) 'If flares go up, lie still!' *'If flares go up, lie still!'* 'Order received! Order received!' 'Up! Up! Up!' The file crawls slowly forward under cover. 'Don't lose touch on the right!' 'Give way on the left!' 'By the right!' *('Cursed squash!' 'Shut your jaw!')* 'Lie down! Lie down! Lie down!' . . .

For a good two hours we lay there on the bare ground. I kept shivering and trying to pull the skirts of my coat over my knees. The man next to me was of course asleep again . . . 'Here, you!' . . . The first flare goes up opposite! Heads down! Of course a few fools must needs look up and watch the damned thing. It slowly dies out. Everything quiet over there. (Are we still so far away that they haven't seen us, or are we under cover?) . . . Pscht! . . . Another one! All dark again. I try, as best I can, to do physical jerks on the ground so as not to get stiff – kick out my legs and so on.

✠ You must know that we are waging three different wars here; one against the lousy Russian; one against the Russian louse (which is now attacking me with greater violence); and – one for the 'Thick' in the camp-kettle! Living in the open of course one gets a tremendous appetite, and when there is pea-soup all the dear comrades fight for the honour of being the one to fetch rations for every eight men. Do you think that is out of Christian charity? Not much! It is the same thing with peas as with people: the empty heads are superficial; those with something in them go deep into the matter, which in the peas' case is the kettle! My partner comes back and sadly announces that he got nothing but 'thin', and to prove it he lets me just look into the can but *not stir it.* Then, very carefully, 'so as not to spill any', he pours the soup into my mess-tin; but I make a quick dive into it and spoon out my share of the 'thick', amid a torrent of abuse from him: 'Greedy pig! No sense of comradeship!' etc. This battle, which is all the fiercer because so far we have only got rations at night, is fought daily, and the same comedy is played everywhere. I, as a young recruit and one who is accustomed to simple student's fare, don't think anything of it; but I wonder how men accustomed to grand table-d'hôte meals in a restaurant feel when they have to join in the battle 'for the thick in the kettle'!

Examine the letters carefully and, as far as possible, find out:

1 Each writer's attitude to war—for example, is there an emphasis on life or death? Are they serious or flippant? Is this necessarily their only attitude?

2 Which letters show the most humour?

3 What do you learn of the writers' personalities?

4 How do they differ in style, e.g. the extent to which they make use of direct speech, use of present tense to describe things in the past, and so on?

5 Which letters would you personally most enjoy receiving?

Truth or Fiction?

**The following letter was written by
Edmund Verney to his son
Edmund, who was away at Mr.
Blackwell's school at Bicester.**

September, 1682

Child,

I received a letter from your master, Mr. Blackwell, who complains of you in your business, and that you are idly and evilly inclined, and particularly that you jointly with some other, as bad as yourself, have lately mischiefed a tablet or two of his, and that you rise in the nights which was made to rest and sleep in . . .

You have much deceived me, your father, who blinded with love to you, thought you no less than a young saint, but now to my grief perceive that you are growing very fast to be an old devil . . .

**The second letter is a model
one such as, it is suggested, children
away from home should write to
their parents. It is taken from**
The Complete Letter-writer, **published
in 1767.**

Dear Papa,

According to your commands, when you left me at School, I hereby obey them; and not only inform you that I am well, but also that I am happy in being placed under the tuition of so good a Master, who is the best natured Man in the World; and I am sure, were I inclinable to be an idle Boy, his goodness to me would prompt me to be diligent at my Study, that I might please him. Besides, I see a great Difference made between those that are idle and those that are diligent, idle Boys being punished as they deserve, and diligent Boys being encouraged. But you know, Papa, that I always loved my Book, for you have often told me, if I intended ever to be a great Man, I must learn to be a good Scholar, lest, when I am grown up, I should be a Laughing-Stock or Make-Game to others, for my Ignorance. But I am resolved to be a Scholar.

Pray give my Duty to my Mamma, and my Love to my Sister.
I am, dear Papa,
Your most dutiful Son.

1   Compare the 'model'
letter with the real one, and
compare the picture we get of the
'model' boy with that of the real
one. Why could neither be
described as an 'average' boy?

2   Work out from the second
letter the personality of the 'dutiful
son' and then write a description of
his day at school so as to shed even
more light on his character.

3 ◄► Write the answer you think
Edmund Verney would send to his
father. You need not copy the
seventeenth-century style of the
original letter.

2 More Formal Letters

There are certain times and occasions when it is customary to send a letter, as for example to express thanks, congratulations or sympathy, or to make an informal invitation to a party.

The conventions lie largely in the actual sending of the letter. The tone of the letter remains on a personal level.

Letters of Thanks

✉ **In the letter below, Alan has not only taken trouble to write and say thank you to his aunt but outlines how he intends to spend the money he has saved.**

98 Lyneham Road,
Luton.
LU2 9JS

18th February 1979

Dear Auntie Mary,

What a marvellous surprise last Monday when I opened the parcel from you and Uncle Ted! I had intended to buy myself a new pair of skates with what I have saved from my pocket money, so they are just what I wanted.

Now I can use the money I had saved towards putting some more fish in the aquarium. You and Uncle Ted can see them when you come here next.

Thanks again for a most acceptable present.

Love, Alan

1 Note the minimum use of formality (address, date, general lay-out, which are basic to <u>all</u> letters).

2 ▪◆ Write a letter of thanks to an aunt or uncle who has sent you a present, which for the second year in succession is totally unsuitable either to your tastes or to your age. (For example, a 'pop' record when you like only classical music, or a pair of stockings when you always wear tights.) Do you just say thank you, or can you drop a diplomatic hint that will remedy the situation another year?

3 ▪◆ Send an informal letter to a friend inviting him or her to a bonfire or birthday or record party. What are the things your guest needs to know from the invitation?

4 ▪◆ Write to congratulate a friend who passed his driving test on the same day as you failed yours.

Putting it into Words:
Letters of Condolence and Sympathy

In some circumstances it is easier to express ourselves by letter than by face-to-face communication or even over the telephone. This is especially true in a difficult or embarrassing situation such as when we wish to convey sympathy or make an apology. Such a letter is of a personal nature and should not sound forced or mechanical. However, there are certain conventions which, if observed, will help you in your writing.

Look at the letter of condolence printed below and you will see what these conventions are.

72 Larks Avenue,
Caerphilly,
Glamorgan.
CF8 2 UA

15th May 1979

Dear Mr and Mrs Johnson,
I would like you to know how deeply sorry I was to hear of John's death after his motor-bike accident last Wednesday.
John had been one of my closest friends since we were at Junior School. He was always cheerful, good tempered, and a good sport. He had a lot of friends because he had time to listen to other people's troubles and to help them.
All John's class-mates wish you to know that we shall not easily forget him, and join me in sending you both all our sympathy.
Yours sincerely,
Kevin Williams

We can now list the conventions which have been followed here.

1   The sending of a letter on such an occasion is customary.

2   Sympathy is expressed in a straightforward and unelaborated manner.

3   Although it would be hypocritical to say things which were not true, it is usual to refer to the good qualities which the dead person possessed.

4   It is not customary to write about any other subject-matter than that which refers to the dead person.

20

Hoping You Get Well Soon

There is a similar set of conventions to follow when writing to people who are ill. But think about the subject-matter of this letter. In a letter of condolence it is only about the person who has died. Why would it be inadvisable in writing to a sick person to dwell only on his illness?

✉ Read the following letter, say how you think it breaks the conventions and then write a letter which would be more appropriate.

22 Chatsworth Road,
Huddersfield.
HD5 3DJ

30 May 1979

Dear Rob,

I was sorry to hear that you'd gone into hospital to have your appendix out. I understand it's rather a tricky operation and you need a long time to recover from it.

Things are happening with a bang at school. It's a pity that you missed the Drama meeting because Miss Whitely chose all the cast for 'Julius Caesar', and I reckon you'd have been sure to get either Caesar or Cassius. I'm playing Brutus and can't wait to get to the assassination scene with the old daggers flashing and all that lovely blood everywhere.

Did you know that we beat Highstones 6-0 last Saturday? Peter Jenkins took over your position and played a great game.

Well, I'd better get on with my homework now. The pressure is really on now as we're doing final revision for the exams. Do you think you'll be back for them?

Exams or no exams, I'm going to make time to see the new James Bond film that's on at the Regal this week.

Hope the moans and groans don't keep you awake at night.

Yours,
Dennis

Opinion and Persuasion

My Point of View

There are several kinds of letter which, because of the personal tone they use, are included in this section rather than the next more formal one. Nevertheless, these are really public letters, aimed at a much wider audience than one particular person.

Let us look first at the letter written by an individual, or a group of people, to be printed in a newspaper. Unless it is just a matter of seeing one's name in print, the writer has something to say about which he feels strongly and on which he believes himself competent to speak.

✉ **Read the letter printed below:**

25th September

Dear Sir,

In a letter published in your paper on Wednesday, 24th September, Mr J. Kilbright complained that to send school-children on party holidays abroad was 'a waste of taxpayers' money'. As I have recently returned from such a trip to Italy I should like to reply to his criticisms.

We first heard about the proposed trip from the Headmaster at the beginning of the Easter term. From this time I worked on a paper-round, getting up at 6 a.m. for seven months, in order to pay for the holiday.

After the party was formed we used to stay behind after school on one evening a week, to have talks and film-shows on what we would see and do in Italy. These meetings really whetted our appetites so that, once abroad, far from 'eating nothing but fish and chips and going to see British films', we were all eager to join in the country's customs and try out its native dishes.

Mr Kilbright also wrote at great length about the behaviour of school parties on the train and boat. I hardly think his remark that children occupy seats while adults are left to stand is a fair one. All our travel bookings were made long before the time of the journey and so we were occupying seats specially reserved for us. Surely on journeys that last many hours everyone should take this precaution of booking seats and cannot complain if, having failed to do this, they are left to stand.

The length of the journey will also account for much of the sweet-eating, 'pop'-drinking, sing-songs and 'parading up and down the corridors' about which your correspondent protests so strongly. Also, it is hardly likely that teenagers, most of whom are travelling abroad for the first time, will manage to bottle up all their excitement and high spirits.

Finally, may I answer the last question which the letter asked, 'What do they learn from it?' For two weeks we were living in another country and joining in a life in many ways different from our own. This taught me that we should respect peoples' differences and be tolerant of them.

I should like to think that Mr Kilbright would be equally tolerant to the young people of this country.

Yours faithfully,
IAN DIXON

124 Linwood Street,
LIVERPOOL.
LI7 9AH

Note the following points:

1   This is a subject about which Ian feels strongly and about which he has something definite to say.

2   The tone of Mr Kilbright's letter was obviously highly intolerant. Ian answers emotion with facts.

3   Although Ian disapproves of Mr Kilbright's attitude he maintains a polite tone throughout.

4   Because Ian is drawing on his own personal knowledge and is not making generalizations, there is an originality about the letter which the newspaper staff will note. There is thus a greater chance that the letter will be published.

Ian's letter answers all the points that Mr Kilbright makes in his letter and it gives some indication of the tone Mr Kilbright adopted.

Make a list of these points and then:

Either Reconstruct Mr Kilbright's letter which he wrote to the newspaper and to which you have just read Ian's reply.

Or   Write a description of one aspect of a school journey. It could be one of the following: the preparation, the journey by train, coach, etc., the first meal, a shopping expedition, a tour of a famous building.

The Power of the Pen

In 1849, Charles Dickens, after watching a public hanging, wrote to The Times about it. This is a slightly edited version of his letter.

Sir,

I was a witness of the public execution at Horsemonger Lane this morning. I believe that a sight so inconceivably awful as the wickedness and levity of the immense crowd could be imagined by no man, and could be presented in no heathen land under the sun. The horrors of the gibbet and of the crime which brought the wretched murderers to it faded in my mind before the atrocious bearing, looks, and language of the assembled spectators. When I came upon the scene at midnight, the shrillness of the cries and howls that were raised from time to time, denoting that they came from a concourse of boys and girls already assembled in the best places, made my blood run cold. As the night went on, screeching, and laughing, and yelling in strong chorus, were added to these. When the day dawned, thieves, low women, ruffians and vagabonds of every kind, flocked on to the ground, with every variety of offensive and foul behaviour. Fightings, faintings, whistlings, imitations of Punch, brutal jokes, tumultous demonstrations of indecent delight when swooning women were dragged out of the crowd by the police, with their dresses disordered, gave a new zest to the general entertainment. When the sun rose brightly – as it did – it gilded thousands upon thousands of upturned faces, so inexpressibly odious in their brutal mirth or callousness, that a man had cause to feel ashamed of the shape he wore, and to shrink from himself, as fashioned in the image of the Devil. When the two miserable creatures who attracted all this ghastly sight about them were turned quivering in the air, there was no more emotion, no more pity, no more thought that two immortal souls had gone to judgment, no more restraint in any of the previous obscenities, than if the name of Christ had never been heard in this world, and there were no belief among men but that they perished like the beasts.

I do not believe that any community can prosper where such a scene of horror and demoralization as was enacted this morning outside Horsemonger Lane Gaol is presented at the very doors of good citizens, and is passed by unknown or forgotten. And I would ask your readers to consider whether it is not a time to think of this moral evil of public execution, and to root it out.

1   What exactly is Dickens protesting against?

2   Whom is he really blaming?

3   List the words and phrases which show the horror and brutality of the scene.

4   What effect do you think Dickens wishes to have on his readers when he describes the unpleasant scene in such detail?

5   What important matters occupy the correspondence columns of our newspapers nowadays?

6 ➡ List the occasions which attract crowds now. Choose one of these and describe the crowd's behaviour. Remember that it will be affected by what the crowd is seeing and hearing, and that it need not be violent or angry.

Selling the Goods

The other type of private/ public letter that we need to examine is the one that sets out to influence in some way.

We have two examples of letters which are both selling, in the first case a product, in the second a person.
First look at the letter from the book firm.

TRANS EUROPA BOOKS LTD

Europa House
60 Grand Street
London W1N 9UZ

Dear Reader,

A few months ago <u>you</u> were one of the thousands of discriminating readers who sent for a copy of our 'History of Flight'.

Now, <u>without any obligation for you to buy</u>, we are giving you a unique opportunity to inspect one of the most exciting books we have ever been privileged to produce.

'PATHWAYS TO THE PLANETS' is a work of which we are justifiably proud. When you examine it for yourself we feel sure you will agree. Here is unfolded the fascinating story of thousands of years, of Man's aspirations, disappointments and triumphs. Read how the Ancients revered the planets. Tread the moon's surface with Armstrong and Aldrin. See how to-day's science fiction becomes to-morrow's reality.

Three hundred and eighty large and colourful pages, lavishly illustrated and luxuriously bound, can be yours to leaf through. Simply answer 'YES' on the enclosed post-card, fill in your name and address and mail it to us. By return of post you will receive this magnificent book.

When you have browsed through it at your leisure you may either return it to us or take advantage of this <u>exclusive offer</u>. If you choose to buy NOW there's an <u>unbelievable 30% discount</u> for you. All you will pay is £3.50, and that includes posting and packing.

But we don't want any money now, just the opportunity to put this truly great book into your hands.

So why not fill in the post-card to-day - we pay the postage - and judge for yourself the quality and value of 'Pathways to the Planets'?

Yours sincerely,

Diane Castle
Diane Castle
(Your personal correspondent)

Note:

1   This letter has obviously been sent out to many thousands of people and yet it has a very personal tone. How many ways can you find in which the letter marks <u>you</u> out?

2   What are the selling points of the offer?

3   What exactly are you being offered? Look at the facts and consider: a. Is it a good buy? b. Is it a book you really would like to own?

4   If you remove the glowing adjectives and adverbs has the offer really lost any of its essential value?

5   Discuss the different devices used to drive home a selling point, for example, types of lettering, paragraphing, etc.

➤   Now compose a letter which will appeal to a wide variety of people in which you offer for sale one of the following:

1   A car-cleaning or baby-sitting service.

2   Hand-made ties.

3   Four years' complete collection of a Hobbies Magazine.

4   An item or service of your own choice.

✉   In the next letter a person is out to sell himself.

402 Porterhouse Street,
MATLOCK,
Derbyshire.
DE4 3BQ
5th November, 1979

Dear Elector,

Your local Independent Party has done me the honour of inviting me to stand as their candidate for the Old Hall Ward in the forthcoming election for the Town Council, and I have the greatest pleasure in accepting the invitation.

I am no stranger to the area, nor indeed to local politics. I was born in Wigmore Street in the Old Hall Ward and, after attending the local primary school, gained a place at Woodmoor Grammar School. Following two years' National Service with the R.A.F., I studied Physics for my degree at Manchester University and also obtained my Teaching Diploma. Since then I have taught in various schools in the town, and for the last three years have been Head of Science at the Crompton Comprehensive School. I am married with two teen-age sons and a nine year-old daughter.

At University I took an active part in student politics. This led me to the firm conclusion that neither of the two main parties can any longer meet the country's needs. What is surely required is a fresh, forceful outlook, not the torrent of tired clichés which constantly flood our ears.

To this end I joined the Independent Party on leaving University, and have been among its most active workers ever since. I was mainly instrumental in formulating our party's policy on Education within the town and helped draft our 'Ten Point Plan on Immigration'.

Now, with your help, I will step out from the wings into the floodlights, to speak on your behalf in the Council Chamber. Education will be my main platform and I will press for equal opportunities for all children, not a privileged few.

If elected, I will investigate closely the proposed rates increase and I will urge a start to the new Ring road.

More houses must be built to reduce the scandalous length of the Housing List. There must be a wide increase in social services to aid the old and lonely, and our youngsters must be given greater facilities to enjoy their leisure time.

IF YOU ARE SATISFIED WITH THE DISGRACEFUL APATHY which characterizes the puny efforts of our present council, then I am *not* your man! If, on the other hand, you count yourself among the thinking members of the electorate, those who care about their town, those who have concern and consideration for their neighbours and families, then I urge you to 'VOTE BLENKINSOP', so that together we may get the job done.

Yours sincerely,

RICHARD BLENKINSOP

Now apply the same criteria as you did in the last letter to decide whether Richard Blenkinsop is 'a good buy'.

For example:

1   What is his relevant political experience and knowledge of the district?

2   What sections of the public is he appealing to? What has he to offer you personally?

3   What positive plans has he to put into effect if elected? For instance, does he say how he will increase social services or what facilities there will be for young people to enjoy?

4   Is the letter free from the 'tired clichés' of which he complains? If not, what examples can you find?

5   To what feelings is the writer appealing in the last paragraph?

▮◆   When you have made up your mind whether you would 'Vote Blenkinsop' or not, write an open letter to persuade people to vote for you on a Staff-Student Council or a Youth Club Committee.

3 Getting Results: Business Letters

We now move on to the more formal types of letter which are generally grouped together as business letters. As well as letters which pass between firms, this group includes letters to book for the theatre and holidays, applications for jobs and references, and letters of complaint.

As there is a marked increase in the formality of the letters from those of the last section, so is there also a similar increase in the use of conventions. Remember that the conventions are used to make things easier for you, and they help to spell out the relationship between you and the person you are writing to. In a given situation, to go against the convention is to put this relationship in jeopardy. A business man may call his golf partner 'Smiler', but if he addresses him in this way and reminds him of their last disastrous game in a letter sent to his firm on business, then both business and friendship may come to a sudden end.

There are three kinds of convention which operate in this section:

1   Lay-out

(a)   As with all letters, the address of the sender and date are written at the top right-hand side of the page.

(b)   Opposite this address is put any reference number the letter may have. (Such a number is used so that all letters dealing with a particular subject may be immediately identifiable.)

(c)   Below the reference number and above the salutation it is usual to write the name and address of the person to whom the letter is being sent, with each line starting at the left-hand margin; or this information may be put at the bottom of the page. There are good reasons for including this. In a large firm with numerous departments and many members of staff a letter might otherwise go astray. Again, it is always advisable for the sender to keep a copy of any such letter, and if it has the name and address of the person to whom it has been sent, it helps to make the filing system work more efficiently.

(d)   The salutation of such letters is either 'Dear Sir', or 'Dear Madam', or 'Dear Sirs', and the subscription is 'Yours faithfully'. If the letter is written on a slightly less formal level, then 'Dear Mr Smith' may be followed by 'Yours sincerely'.

The signature must be written legibly and, in the case of a woman, 'Miss' or 'Mrs' must be added in brackets after the signature.

2   Contents

Do not introduce other matters: keep to the subject.

3   Style

Be as concise and clear as possible. Introduce your subject at once, then develop details of this subject in the main body of your letter. See how Sir Philip Sidney, writing four hundred years ago, acts on his opening sentence, 'Few words are best'. There is no fear of the point of his letter being lost under the weight of unnecessary words.

1578, Philip Sidney to Edward Molyneux:

Mr Molyneux,

Few words are best. My letters to my father have come to the eyes of some. Neither can I condemn any other but you for it. If it be so, you have played the very knave with me: and so I will make you know if I have good proof of it. But that for so much as is past. For that is to come, I assure you before God, that if ever I know you do so much as read any letter I write to my father, without his commandment, or my consent, I will thrust my Dagger into you. And trust to it, for I speak in earnest. In the meantime farewell.

From Court this last of May 1578,
By me
PHILIP SIDNEY

Making it Plain

Letters which fall into this group, which you may often be called upon to write, are those to make reservations or to buy some product by post as advertised in the Press. In both cases, you will be dealing with a large amount of information and so you should aim at two things : Accuracy and Ordering —to write down all the required information in a well-ordered way so that there will be no misunderstanding or delays in getting what you have asked for.

Look at the following request for theatre tickets and note that although a large number of details have to be given the letter remains concise and straightforward.

13 Bannister Street,
PRESTON.
PR1 2JD

1st February, 1979

The Box Office,
Queen's Theatre,
Market Street,
MANCHESTER.
M1 8DH

Dear Sirs,
    Please find enclosed a stamped addressed envelope and cheque for £6·00, for four seats at £1·50 reserved by telephone today, for the 7.30 p.m. performance of 'Romeo and Juliet', on Friday, 21st February.
                    Yours faithfully,
                    R. P. COPE

Things to Do

1 ▪▶ **Hugh Porter wants to book
a holiday for himself and his
friend. All the details are given
below, but not in an ordered way.
Put them in order, and write the
letter Hugh should send.**

Dates of holiday:	9—30 June.
Names of people booking:	Hugh Porter and Barry Skinner.
Name and address of Tourist Agency:	Safari North Africa, 500 North Street, Croydon. CR0 9LA
Request made by Hugh:	List of essential items of clothing and camping equipment.
Deposit of £25 per person required:	Hugh encloses cheque for £25.
Barry's address:	135 Lenton Road, Hull. HU4 7LF
Places Safari visits:	Morocco, Algeria, and Libya.
Length of holiday:	Three weeks.
Hugh's address:	13 Cottingham Avenue, Willerby, Hull. HU10 6EW
Date of Hugh's letter:	12th March 1979.

2 ▪▶ **An important politician or
entertainment personality has
promised to give a talk to your
Youth Club. Write to his (or her)
secretary to make final
arrangements about the date,
time and length of the talk, and
give instructions on how to reach
the club.**

3 **Choose an advertisement
from a newspaper or magazine for
a product you would like. Write the
appropriate letter to obtain this.
Remember (a) to quote the
newspaper in which you saw the
advertisement, and (b) to give the
number and amount of any Postal
Order enclosed.**

First Impressions: Applying for a Job

A letter of application is usually the first contact you have with a prospective employer. The aim of this letter is to show why you should be chosen from among the other applicants for the job.

✉ Read the following answers to the advertisement below, and select two candidates to go forward for interview.

Give reasons for <u>all</u> of your decisions.

When you exclude an applicant make your reasons for doing so clear.

In some cases, the personality of the writer is evident. Where is this not the case and why?

TRAINEE REPORTER

Applications are invited from school leavers for the post of trainee reporter on the staff of the Purley Mercury. Applicants should possess a good command of written English and have at least four C.S.E. subjects. Apply by letter to the Editor, Purley Mercury, 100 South Street, Purley, Surrey, CR2 4TJ.

Evening Mercury, 26 June 1979

---

20 High Trees,
CROYDON.
CR0 7UR

27th June, 1979

The Editor,
The Purley Mercury,
100 South Street,
PURLEY,
Surrey.
CR2 4TJ

Dear Sir,

I saw your advertisement for a traineee reporter in yesterday's Purley Mercury. I should like to be considered for the post. I am captain of the school football team and play centre forward for my youth club team who won last year's championship. We hope to repeat our performance this year. I am sixteen and have taken five subjects to C.S.E. level – English, History, French, Metalwork and Mathematics.

I want to do well and feel sure that I would be able to do a good job.

Yours sincerely,

THOMAS PARSONS

15 Elmgrove Road,
CROYDON.
CR0 7DQ

28th June, 1979

The Editor,
The Purley Mercury,
100 South Street,
PURLEY,
Surrey.
CR2 4TJ

Dear Sir,

I wish to be considered for the post of reporter advertised in the Purley Mercury on Wednesday evening.

I have the required educational qualifications, having taken seven C.S.E. subjects. I have edited the School Magazine for the last two years.

I am able to be interviewed on either Thursday afternoons or Saturday mornings. In your reply please indicate the prospects of promotion, and salary scales which are appropriate to this post.

My form mistress and my father's bank manager have agreed to provide you with references. Their addresses are:

Miss K. P. Davies,
Glynn House,
Riverside Lane,
Arlingham,
GLOUCESTER.
GL2 7YZ

P. Scott-Wilson,
42 Homer Road,
CROYDON.
CR0 7SB

I look forward to hearing from you at your earliest convenience.

Yours faithfully,

JOANNA O. HALLAM

---

31 Mint Walk,
CROYDON.
CR0 1EA

1st July, 1979

The Editor,
The Purley Mercury,
100 South Street,
PURLEY,
Surrey.
CR2 4TJ

Dear Sir,

I wish to apply for the post advertised in the Purley Mercury. I have taken four C.S.E. subjects and I am leaving school in three weeks' time.

Yours in anticipation,

J. QUICK

24 Hillcroft Avenue,
PURLEY,
Surrey.
CR2 3DG

27th June, 1979

The Editor,
The Purley Mercury,
100 South Street,
PURLEY,
Surrey.
CR2 4TJ

Dear Sir,

With regard to your advertisement for the post of trainee reporter on the staff of the Purley Mercury, which appeared in last night's issue, I should like to be considered for the post.

I am sixteen years old and in my last year at Dewey Secondary School. I have taken the following subjects in my C.S.E. examinations – English, Mathematics, History, Geography, French, Biology. I hope to continue my Shorthand and Typing classes at Evening School.

For the last school year I have been House Vice-captain and my main sporting interests are football and swimming.

I have taken an interest in the work of editing the School Magazine for the last two issues and before that I helped in the production of a form news sheet.

I give below the names and addresses of people who will act as my referees should you require them.

J. P. Masters, B.A.,   Mrs Irene Thomas, J.P.,
15 Clovelly Avenue,   501 East Street,
WARLINGHAM,   MITCHAM,
Surrey.   Surrey.
CR3 9HZ   CR4 4RS

I look forward to hearing from you,
Yours sincerely,
JAMES G. PHILLIPS

Giving a Reference

In the previous section two of the applicants for the job on the Purley Mercury **give the names of people who will act as <u>referees</u> for them. This means that the Editor of the** Mercury **may <u>refer</u> to these people to learn more about the applicants' personality and suitability for the job. What they say or write is known as a <u>reference.</u>**

Most jobs require references, so it is best to understand what this entails. When you ask a person to act as your referee you are wanting him or her to speak favourably on your behalf. You must realize, though, that if references are to be of any value they must be a true record of what the referee thinks and knows about you. Thus it would be of little use to give the name of your vicar if you never attend his church. Nor do relations act as referees because it is thought unlikely that they could give an unbiased opinion.

While you are at school your Head or Form teacher is an obvious choice for referee. If a second reference is required you could ask someone who knows you well out of school.

Remember that people acting as your referees are doing you a favour, because they will be giving time and thought to what they will say about you. It is therefore essential and indeed only common politeness that you always ask a person to be your referee <u>before</u> you put his name forward to your prospective employer, and it is also a nice gesture to let him know if your job application has been successful.

Study the reference below that J. P. Masters wrote on behalf of James Phillips.

15 Clovelly Avenue,
WARLINGHAM,
Surrey.
CR3 9HZ

8th July, 1979

The Editor,
The Purley Mercury,
100 South Street,
PURLEY,
Surrey.
CR2 4TJ

Dear Sir,

I shall be very pleased to write on behalf of James Phillips whom I have known for the five years he has been a pupil at Dewey Secondary School. I have taught him English for four of these years and I have been his form-master for the last ten months.

James is a hard-working boy who has achieved a good all-round standard. He is particularly strong in English and History. In the former subject his work shows imagination and he is an avid reader. His written work is accurately and neatly presented and he has proved an able speaker in Inter-House debates.

James possesses a number of qualities which should fit him for the post of trainee reporter. He is observant and willing to listen and take advice. His work on the school Magazine and class news-sheet has demonstrated well these qualities. A popular boy with both staff and pupils at school, James would, I feel sure, gain the confidence of the people he worked with in the office and those he interviewed on the newspaper's behalf.

If you have any special questions you wish to ask about James I shall be glad to answer them.

Yours faithfully,
J. P. MASTERS (B.A.)

Now imagine that one of your class-mates has asked you to act as his or her referee for one of the jobs on the next page. Write the reference, making full use of what you know of your class-mate's qualifications, personality and suitability for the job.

☛ **Read the following advertisements and write a letter of application to the one that interests you most.**

SIR JOSEPH ERNLEY AND PARTNERS

require

FIRST-CLASS PERSON TO BRING THEIR OFFICE TEAM UP TO SCRATCH

What we need is
- A junior Secretary, age about 18

What we offer is
- A pleasant, friendly atmosphere in modern surroundings
- A 35-hour week
- Luncheon vouchers
- An excellent salary with regular reviews
- Life assurance and pension schemes

WRITE – TODAY!

Moss House, 70 Great Queen Street, LONDON WC2B 5BB

LABORATORY ASSISTANT. We are one of the largest and most rapidly expanding self-contained producers of chromium carbide based tools in the country. We wish to train a young man or woman in our chemical laboratory. Applicants should have qualifications in science subjects. Write to: Hume Alloys Ltd., Fullbrook Road, WALSALL WS5 4NT

MOTHER'S HELP to look after Miranda 1½ years, and baby due in August. Suit school-leaver. Own room, television. Generous free time. Good wages. Write with full details to Mrs. J. Cooke, 12 Cornish Crescent, BATH BA1 2DX

MODEL. Experience not essential, required for fashion house near Oxford Circus. 35 in. hip. A knowledge of either typing or switchboard could be an advantage. Apply Mandy, Andre Stevens Originals Ltd., 620 Oxford Street, LONDON W1C 4KK

REQUIRED IMMEDIATELY. School leaver to train as sales person in our Sports Department. We are looking for someone keen who can handle people and money, and who knows about sport. Excellent starting wage and staff pension scheme. Apply in writing to The Staff Manager, Freebody and Tomkins Ltd., 9 High Street, HULL HU1 1HF

CORDOS Limited
Young Men and Women

Here's your chance to enter advertising

Cordos Limited, one of Europe's biggest agencies is looking for people between 16 and 18 who want to start their careers in advertising.

- You'll work in media initially, but the chances are you'll move around and earn promotion pretty quickly.

- You'll need an ordered mind, the ability to communicate, and you'll probably have Maths and English at C.S.E. level, Grade 1 or 2.

- We can offer you good money, plenty of extra benefits, and a very friendly atmosphere to work in.

So, if you're going to grab this chance, just write to: Cordos Limited
Cordos House
250 Fleet Street,
LONDON.
EC4A 2JN

Any Complaints?

These are the letters that we all feel the need to write sooner or later. In writing them, we should ask ourselves whether the aim is merely to complain, to let off steam, or is it to achieve something more positive; for example, a refund of money, the replacement of damaged or imperfect goods, or something similar? If the latter is intended, then we must handle the situation tactfully. It is worth bearing the following points in mind:

1   Most firms will respond to genuine complaints which are expressed in reasonable terms. The common idea that getting things done inevitably requires excessive rudeness is an unreliable guide to writing letters which aim at coping with this sort of situation.

2   Even when there is the protection of a guarantee, a letter may be necessary to set things in motion. Besides this, a written record of what has gone wrong, bearing a date, is always useful, as the guarantee may run out before the matter has been settled.

3   More than one letter may be necessary. It pays to be persistent.

4   As a general rule, most large firms wish to avoid unflattering publicity of any kind. This means that as a last resort there is always the option of writing to local or national newspapers. It is quite usual for some papers and radio and television programmes to adopt the grievances and complaints of ordinary citizens and to take them up on their behalf.

5   <u>Never</u> threaten legal proceedings. If you should reach the stage where this seems necessary, get a solicitor to write on your behalf.

6   Always keep a copy of this and any other type of business letter, and make sure you know where to find it. Use a cardboard file, a large envelope or a bulldog clip for this purpose.

e.g. You have bought an expensive dress labelled 'Washable' in a sale at a greatly reduced price. After a while it is washed and the colours run. What do you do? As is often the case, the shop where you bought the dress points out that sale goods are not returnable. On the face of it, everything indicates that you have to make the best of a bad job.

39

This is a situation where it might pay to bank on the firm in question being sufficiently jealous of its reputation to offer some compensation, and you might compose a letter on the following lines.

25 Pentrefelin Road,
MOLD,
Flintshire.
CH7 3YA

March 25th, 1979

The Sales Director,
Fashion Ltd.,
27 Swansea Road,
NEWPORT,
Monmouthshire.
NPT 2RT

Dear Sir,

On January 6th this year I made a special journey to Manchester for the Sales.

From the Fashion Department of Cranmore's in Buckfast Street I bought a blue and white dress, in your 'Gresham' range, marked down from sixteen pounds to three. As I have always admired your clothing I was very pleased with my buy.

Before buying the dress, as it was slightly soiled, I asked the assistant if it was washable or must it be dry-cleaned. She showed me the label inside the collar which clearly stated, 'Hand wash. Cool iron'.

With this assurance I bought the dress and, after wearing it three times, I started to wash it, quite separately from any other clothing. I was horrified to see that there was a considerable amount of blue dye coming out of it into the water and, in spite of repeated rinsings and careful drying, the blue ran into the white parts of the dress.

I wrote to Cranmore's telling them that the dress was ruined. They replied regretting what had happened, but declined to do anything further as the dress was sales goods and therefore money could not be refunded on it.

I am now left with a relatively new dress which cannot be worn any more and feel doubly upset because it has come from a firm of your high standing.

I would appreciate it if you would give time to investigating why this particular dress carried a label with false information on it, and then to consider if I might be recompensed for being the victim of this error.

I will be happy to send you the dress if you wish to examine it.

I look forward to an early reply from you.

Yours faithfully,

MARY WHITING (Miss)

Note:

1   The letter gives precise details of the date and place of purchase.

2   It gives an exact description of the dress—maker's name and model of dress, washing instructions, etc.

3   The general tone of the letter conveys surprise and disappointment, rather than annoyance and rudeness.

4   The onus is now on the dress firm to investigate the complaint to safeguard its good reputation.

■◆ Now do the following:
You are getting a very fuzzy picture on your TV set. The rental company has fitted a new aerial for which you have paid, but the picture has not improved. In spite of repeated telephone calls, you can gain no satisfaction. Write the letter which you think will bring results.

Saying What You Mean

In writing business letters some people are guilty of sending out letters which sound very stilted indeed. This is because they are using expressions and terms which were once conventional, but which are so out-dated that often they hinder rather than help a ready understanding of the letter's contents.

✉ The following is a clear example of such a letter.

ULTRA-MELLOTONE GUITARS LIMITED
24 Little Titchfield Street
London W1P 7FH

14th February 1979

G. E. Lewis, Esq.,
27 South Street,
LLANTWIT MAJOR,
Glamorgan.
CF6 9LT

Dear Client,

    We thank you for your valued communication of the 12th inst., in which you inform us of the accident and resulting damage to your Rhapsody guitar. May we, however, respectfully draw your attention to Clause XIV, section ii, of your agreement with us, according to which the responsibility for damage of this type resides with owner.

    In the event that your private insurance arrangements do not cover this situation, may we suggest that you take advantage of our speedy repair service in our own specially designed workshop where our professionally trained craftsmen, using the most up-to-date machine tools provide a first class service. All repairs undertaken carry our personal guarantee.

    Assuring you of the best of our attention at all times,

        We remain,

        Yours faithfully,

Miles Gillard

        Miles Gillard,
        Sales Manager,
        Ultra-Mellotone Guitars Ltd.

Note:

1   Phrases like 'Valued communication', and 'Resides with owner' lack directness and originality. They belong to an old-fashioned business jargon. Find other similar phrases in the letter and make up better ways of expressing them.

2   The phrases 'May we', 'respectfully', 'valued communication', 'assuring you' give the impression that the firm is only too anxious to please their client. But does what they are telling the client really uphold this impression?

Silk **Hair Products Ltd.**

Gainsborough House . Belsize Avenue . London N13 4JL

Ref : JCP/PD   10th September 1979

Dear Madam,

              'Silklight' Hair Lotion

      We are in receipt of your letter of the 28th ult. and the parcel containing the bottle of 'Silklight' hair lotion which you have returned.

      We deeply regret that you failed to achieve the desired results, but would draw your attention to what we feel sure are instrumental factors in the results you describe.

      1. Specific instructions are given which must be followed exactly.

      2. Hair which has been previously lightened by another proprietary brand will not respond satisfactorily to our lotion.

      3. General debility in the health of the user can give rise to dull and lifeless hair, in which case, satisfactory results are hardly to be expected from our lotion.

We cannot emphasise too strongly that all our products are scientifically tested in the most stringent laboratory conditions. Moreover, we receive annually thousands of letters of commendation from delighted customers expressing their total satisfaction. It is our sincere hope therefore that this letter has given you renewed confidence in us and that you will continue to use our products in the future.

      Assuring you of our best service at all times,

              We remain,

              Your obedient servant,

              Jacqueline C. Foreman

              Jacqueline C. Foreman
              Hair Counsellor.

Miss Susan Pettit,
32 Dunstan Road,
WELLS,
Somerset.   BA5 6LH

1   On the surface, this letter appears polite. Which words and phrases give this impression?

2   In fact, it is a rude letter which aims at putting Susan in the wrong. Find examples of this.

3   List all the examples of old-fashioned business jargon you can find. Do they always mean here what they say?

4 ✎➤ Re-write the letter in such a way that the firm will not lose Susan's custom.

43

4 A Matter of Form

In the final section we have the most formal type of letter, used for invitations and acceptances for formal occasions such as weddings, banquets and so on. We are now as far as possible from the relative freedom of the personal letter.

The custom has been established that the layout, wording, and presentation as a whole follow a definite pattern.

This form of invitation and reply is used most often where large numbers of people are concerned, and is frequently in the form of a printed card. The persons giving the invitation want the information on it expressed clearly so that there is no danger of misunderstanding on the reader's part. Replies worded in the agreed customary way may be quickly read, and acceptances or refusals noted.

✉ **Study how the following wedding invitation and reply are worded and set out. In particular, notice the following features:**

1   The impersonal tone is emphasized by the fact that the invitation is written in the third person.

2   The reply repeats most of the information in the invitation as a means of reassuring the host that his guest has understood and noted the exact time, place, and other relevant details.

3   If an invitation is refused, a reason must be given briefly.

Mr. and Mrs. J. F. Robins
request the pleasure of the company of
Mrs M. Wells and Mr J. Wells
at the marriage of their daughter
Josephine Anne to Mr. James Ford
at St. Neot's Church, Shepton Mallet
on Saturday, 6th of June at 11 a.m.,
and afterwards at the Tudor Arms Hotel,
Rocksdale Road, Shepton Mallet

R.S.V.P. — The Hollies,
Barton Square, Shepton Mallet,
Somerset BA4 3BD

Mrs Mary Wells is pleased to accept the invitation of Mr & Mrs J. F. Robins to the wedding of their daughter, Josephine Anne and Mr James Ford, at St Neot's Church, Shepton Mallet, on Saturday, 6th of June, and afterwards at the Tudor Arms Hotel.

She regrets that John is unable to accept as he will be abroad at the time.

It is by no means an infallible rule that only this type of reply is acceptable, and such letters may be worded in a more informal manner.

Mrs Wells might write:

✉

10 PARSONAGE STREET
SHEPTON MALLET
SOMERSET
BA4 6BE

14th May 1979

Dear Mrs Robins,

    I shall be very pleased to accept your kind invitation to Josephine's wedding on June 6th at St Neot's church, and to the reception at the Tudor Arms Hotel.

    Unfortunately, John will be in Germany at the time and so won't be able to attend.

    Yours sincerely,

    Mary Wells.

1 ◀ Imagine that your class is organizing a large Christmas party. Write the formal invitation to your head teacher.

2 ◀ You have been formally invited to a friend's birthday party. Write your reply.

46

More Things to Do

1 ▮◆ Imagine you are working overseas. Invent your own job, choose a place, and write a letter home. Try to bring in as much information as you can by using different sources such as atlases, guidebooks, etc.

2 When people in public life resign they often have their letter of resignation published in the newspapers. Can you think of any reasons why they should do this? Find some examples of such letters for discussion in class. You can find a copy of Winston Churchill's letter of resignation, published in The Times on 13 November 1915, in Alan Moorhead's Churchill: A Pictorial Biography.

3 Discuss why pen-friendships rarely last.

4 Why do people on holiday send postcards, and what do they usually say?

5 ▮◆ Write one of the following letters:
(a) to an embassy for information on a project in the country in question.
(b) to a factory/library/farm/zoo/newspaper office, etc., arranging for a visit by a party from school.

6 ▮◆ You have cut down the branches of a tree in next door's garden which grew over on your side and made the kitchen dark. Your neighbour is now refusing to speak to you. Write him/her a letter of apology.

7 ▮◆ Write to the Radio Times or T.V. Times either to criticize or to praise a programme or television personality you have seen this week.

8 Collect all the letters which appear in your newspaper for a week. Study them and find out the following: what subjects they discuss, the points of view they take, the ways in which they present those views.

9 ▮◆ Write to the local offices of the major political parties, asking them whether they can send you any copies of election addresses. Study them and see how they compare with Blenkinsop's letter in this book.

10 Collect examples of official letters (e.g. Inland Revenue, National Health, local Council, etc.) and see whether they express themselves in a readily understandable way.

11 ➤ Reply to the following invitation:

The Mayor and Corporation
of Leigh-on-Sea
request the pleasure of the company of

....

at a Banquet to be held in the Town Hall
on Saturday 12th December at 7.30 p.m.

R.S.V.P. – Mayor's Parlour,
Town Hall, Crescent Road,
Leigh-on-Sea, Essex SS9 2PS

Dress formal

---

12   Discuss when a telephone or some other means of communication would be preferable to sending a letter.